The Secret Self

The Secret Self

Orlo Strunk, Jr.

Abingdon
Nashville

THE SECRET SELF

Copyright © 1976 by Abingdon

Library of Congress Cataloging in Publication Data

Strunk, Orlo.
   The secret self.
   1. Self. 2. Secrecy (Psychology) I. Title.
BF697.S87   158′.1   76-14780

ISBN 0-687-37299-2

Scripture quotations are from the Revised Standard Version of the Bible, copyrighted 1946, 1952, and 1971, by the Division of Christian Education, National Council of Churches, and are used by permission.

"Your Eyes Have Put Me in a File" by Orlo Strunk, Jr., is reprinted from *Pilgrimage: The Journal of Pastoral Psychotherapy* (Spring-Summer, 1974).

Steven Kull's Evening Review is reprinted from *Synthesis*, The Realization of the Self, vol. I, no. 1, 830 Woodside Road, Suite 5, Redwood City, Calif. 94061.

"Experimental Prayer" by Orlo Strunk, Jr., is copyright © 1974 by The United Methodist Publishing House and is reprinted from *United Methodists Today* (January, 1975).

"Children" by Ethel Romig Fuller is reprinted from *Kitchen Sonnets* by permission of the publisher, Binfords & Mort.

MANUFACTURED BY THE PARTHENON PRESS AT
NASHVILLE, TENNESSEE, UNITED STATES OF AMERICA

TO
The Fathers and Brothers
of the
Province of St. Paul of the Cross
(Passionists)

Preface

My reason for writing this book has its origin in my desire to share some feelings and insights about the Self which have come to me over the past ten years. There is a centerpoint in all of us which belongs to us. It does not belong in the public domain. It is private. Even secret. Often very silent. And this, I maintain, can be a good and very important thing.

In one sense what I am saying is reactionary, because much in our times encourages the opposite—even *requires* the opposite: that we be public, fully and completely. In one of the communities in which I move—the psychotherapeutic community—this tendency to be public in all things is frequently presented as a given, a fact beyond argument. I do not accept this argument, however, and this book is partly an explanation of why I cannot buy into the emphasis on making ourselves fully public.

Much of what is expressed here has been generated out of a complex of experiences and roles—as a husband and father, a college and university professor, a clergyman, an educational administrator, a psychologist, and a counselor. And, frankly, it surely has some of its roots in a simple developmental fact: I have passed the mid-life point!

My hope for this book is a simple one: I want it to say something helpful to others who may be experiencing transitions of one kind or another; and I want it to provide a friendly context for reflecting on the nature and development of the secret Self in relation to these transitions.

I am well aware that much of what I write in this primer is elementary. I do not write it for the professional mystic or the experienced spiritual guide. It is a kind of informal conversation I might have with anyone, young or old, who is sensing a transition in his or her life and is beginning to wonder if there is not "something more." I believe there is always something more, and that the secret Self holds one of the keys to such expansive realities.

Although much of what I am writing about here stems from my own experiences, there is certainly a real sense in which every book, like every person, is dependent upon a variety of individuals. In the case of this volume, I want to express my debt to the following: to Martha Crampton, Director of the

Canadian Institute of Psychosynthesis, for helping me to experience some of the ideas outlined in this book; to Fr. Kevin Culligan, O.C.D., whose own attempts meaningfully to relate modern psychotherapy and ancient spiritual direction have sensitized me to a wider therapeutic vision; and to the many priests and brothers of the Province of St. Paul of the Cross, to whom the book is dedicated, who allowed me, a Protestant minister-psychologist, to poke around in their monasteries and minds, which made it possible for me to grasp at first hand how very human the spiritual can be and how deeply spiritual is the human.

Orlo Strunk, Jr.

Contents

"There is a centerpoint in all of us which belongs to us. It does not belong in the public domain. It is private. Even secret. Often very silent."

1.

The Person You Are

You are a person. This means that you are more than a body, more than a mind, more than a man or a woman. You are more than a schoolteacher or a farmer or a mother or a son or a daughter. And you are more than an American or a Canadian or a Frenchman. You may be a Catholic or a Protestant or a Muslim or an atheist, but you are much much more than any one of these or any combination of them put together. You are a person.

Any time people see you as a role or a function, they are not seeing you as a person. And any time you see another as a function or as a one-dimensional thing, you are not seeing him or her as a person.

I recall several years ago interviewing a young woman who had come to me for counseling. As I listened to her story and watched her eyes and hands, I felt strangely uncomfortable. She was directing words at me, but somehow the words seemed wooden and worn. So strong was my feeling, that after she left I wrote the following on the back of the form containing the interview notes:

> Your eyes have put me in a file.
> You have alphabetized me like a punched card;
>   and now, content, you relax and ask to be
>   raped by the numbers.
> How strange that you should make a white page
>   from a gray suit and a red tie!
> Look closer. Don't you see the life around my eyes?
> Don't you see the silent throbbing of the blue vein
>   just above my index finger?
> No, you don't see. You are wide-eyed and blind,
>   and you think you need a punched card
>   filed away.[1]

I did not write this to blame my client for failing to see me as a person, for she was under stress and was naturally preoccupied with herself at the time; and she surely felt she needed a professional. Rather, I wrote it to try to capture the feeling I experienced as a result of being seen as a professional, in this instance as a psychologist. Most of us have this kind of experience a dozen times a day. And most of us tend to see others this way as well. What is happening is that we fail to see others as persons.

Much has been written about what a person is, including some complex assortments of difficult theories. But I have found that the best way to answer

[1] *Pilgrimage: The Journal of Pastoral Psychotherapy* (Spring-Summer, 1974), p. 49.

the question is a subjective one: to start from what I believe myself to be as a person, and then to assume that others must have similar qualities or expectations. If I, for example, hope that another person might relate to me as more than a professional, is it not possible that the other person might hope that I would see him or her as more than a "patient" or a "client" or a "case"? I think so.

Because of our busy days we easily accept shorthand ways of dealing with persons. This appears inevitable. We can, however, keep a check on ourselves to see if we appreciate the full dimensionality of the person before us. Are our short-cut dealings allowing us to be present to the other, even if only for the few minutes of our meeting and encounter? Are we aware that this encounter is not simply the meeting of two things or objects but ideally and potentially of two persons in touch with one another, both complex human beings?

Part of this issue centers on our own expectations as persons. We have a right to expect others to meet us as persons, and this is true whether one is the president of the corporation or the person who empties the executives' wastebaskets. This is not something we need to earn. It is given to us as humans. It is part of the secret Self, part of what is at the center of you and me. The expectation is not only legitimate, it is an imperative. To expect less is to claim that you are less than human.

Recently a client of mine told me how he and his

17

wife had gone to a bank to secure an automobile loan. The interviewer was aloof and rude. My client sensed that the banker didn't like his long hair, and noticed that he avoided even looking at his wife, a Puerto Rican.

"Why didn't you ask the interviewer why he was treating you this way?" I asked my client.

Several days later this young man told me that my question had stimulated him to go back and confront the banker with his feelings about the interview. After some embarrassed stammering, the young banker admitted that he had been curt and impolite. "It was a busy and difficult day," he explained, "and I thought, 'I'll get rid of these hippies in a hurry.'"

My client felt better after telling the banker that he and his wife were persons and deserved better treatment. And I suspect that the young banker felt something, too, and perhaps through open discussion grew a bit more as an interviewer and as a person.

Of course, it is difficult for us to think of ourselves and others as persons all the time. But if the quality of life is to improve, this is what must be done.

Holding to Rich Meanings of Persons

We are often prevented from fully appreciating the worth of the person by our desire to simplify ourselves and others. A whole society tries to make us believe that we are all pretty much alike. One of the main reasons we like to paste a label on people or put them in a category is that such a practice gives us a feeling of being in control. If we can find a word that will sum up another person's behavior, we use it to give us relief from a sense of ambiguity or mystery.

In my own profession I frequently come up against this sort of verbal magic. At a staff conference a case will be presented. A massive amount of information about a person will come forth, and peculiar behavior will be described in great detail. How can we understand this person's strange behavior? Finally someone may say, "Well, it is clear that he is a passive-aggressive individual," and a common sigh will sweep across the room, shoulders will relax, a calmness will move in to replace confusion. The magic of a word has worked again.

It is difficult to imagine just how destructive this kind of stereotyping can be unless you yourself have been the target of such verbal gymnastics. Have you ever had another person interrupt your struggle to explain yourself or an idea with the words "I know, you're a Republican" or "Say no more, you're a typical Irishman!" or "That's what I'd expect from a father"?

At times such oversimplified summaries have cut into me painfully. The words had little to do with any serious attempt to understand me; rather, they were called forth to give security to the speaker. And although I can appreciate the need for such an illusion of understanding and control, I cannot believe that such an understanding is worth it.

The psychologists have a term which is helpful here: *premature closure*—by which they mean our natural tendency to turn what is incomplete into something complete. If we are shown an incomplete circle in a hurried way, we will call it a circle even though it is not truly a circle, or not yet anyway. You and I both *like* to do this. It is a way we have of rounding out our world, of keeping things neat and orderly. But it is just what the term says, *premature*.

The danger in such a procedure is that we oversimplify ourselves and others. By engaging in premature closure we wipe out the fullness of the other person. In an effort to make things simple and complete, we prostitute the authenticity of personhood. Often this gives us a false sense of living and understanding. We miss the richness of the other person, not because it is absent, but because our own need for closure blinds us to the fullness of reality.

One way to correct this fractured way of seeing others and ourselves is to hold to the rich meanings of persons. The many dimensions of personhood are complex and intertwined. Denial will not change this; it will only provide a false security and an illusion which will prevent us from coming to know the richness implicit in the world.

We do not need to be philosophers to acknowledge the rich meanings of persons, although reading philosophy may be one way of sensitizing us to this cornucopia of meaning. We have only to look within, to examine quietly our motives and beliefs, to reassess our priority of *time* (a factor to be considered in greater detail in a later chapter).

What makes you aware that as a person you have many dimensions? Perhaps you, like me, are brought to this point when you are misunderstood, when others draw conclusions about you which you know very well are false or overly simple.

A few weeks ago I was having lunch with a young man who was contemplating doing graduate work. We had never met before. After some simple chitchat, we got down to specific and practical matters, and soon it became obvious to me that Ron was talking around the issues. Since we had only an hour for our conversation, I decided to be blunt.

"Look, Ron, you still haven't told me about your long-term objective. Maybe if I knew that I could be more helpful in suggesting a program for you."

Ron sipped his iced tea, squirmed a bit in his chair. "Well, Dr. Strunk, I'm really interested in prison reform. Last year I worked as a volunteer in a prison, and I'm convinced that job's where I'd like to serve."

When I asked Ron why he was hesitant about sharing this with me, he said, "Believe it or not, it was your haircut. I mean, after all, who wears their hair short like that?"

"Except maybe an Archie Bunker," I added.

Ron nodded. "I don't know your views on prison reform, but your hair and your age tell me that you're

21

probably a 'law and order' type who would resist real reform."

"As to the hair," I explained, "you should have seen me three weeks ago! The fact is, Ron, I get my hair cut short for the summer months when I'm out in the sun and water. During the winter I let it grow. It has to do with comfort, not politics. As for my age, my control is limited."

The conversation then shifted into a humorous vein. Both of us were able to talk about stereotyping. As we talked, Ron found that some of my views on prison reform were too radical and unrealistic. For my part, I discovered that Ron's attempt to freeze me into the middle-aged box was partly based on experiences he had recently had in talking with another university professor. Within a brief hour we both learned a bit more about each other, far more than if we had judged each other by appearance alone.

Yet it would be naïve to claim that the physical dimension of personhood is unimportant. It remains true, for instance, that clothing is often a key to how a person sees himself or herself. Clothing often is one expression of selfhood. It is an extension of the person. Where we hit a reef is in assuming that the relationship between person and clothing is a simple one and settling for a superficial understanding. Even more dangerous is the quiet and often unexamined conviction that a particular physical characteristic, including clothing, has but one meaning. Driven by the need for closure, we jump to our favorite

22

conclusion and never know just how wrong we are. To settle for such a terribly poor imitation of the reality of the person surely makes life into a cardboard stage peopled by simple, unexciting actors.

Oversimplifying the physical dimension is only one way in which we fail to appreciate the many dimensions of the person. We frequently do the same when dealing with the minds of our fellow creatures. In fact, our need for closure here can be especially destructive to the idea of full personhood. The human mind is a rich crucible of ideas, memory, and imagination. As I reflect on it here at my writing desk, I am overcome by its complexity and richness. I really do not know where to start. For the most part, man's mind is an unexplored universe, complex and fathomless. What a travesty when we permit ourselves to perceive it in simple terms or think that it involves only intellect.

Some years ago my wife and I were visiting a young couple recently graduated from a college I knew very well. Some of the young men and women I had known in former years were still there working on their studies. The young couple had a yearbook, and together we searched through the volume making comments about familiar faces. It suddenly dawned on me that our host and hostess invariably characterized the students in terms of intellect or of academic achievement: "Oh, was he ever a dull one!" "She was strictly a C student, you know." "Remember

23

Tom, the basketball player? You had to point him in the direction of the door after the bell rang."

Both these young people were bright, and eager to do graduate studies. They were themselves the children of university professors. It was natural that they should place great value on the intellectual dimension. But what a shame that they did not allow themselves to experience the richness of personhood! Intellect, after all, is only one mini-dimension of the mind, let alone of the person.

Consider for a moment your own imagination. Its power is enormous and creative—and it is yours. You may choose to share it with others. But it is yours to play with, if you so desire.

Yesterday as I was driving into the city I noticed that the car in front of me had a bumper sticker which read: I'D RATHER BE FISHING. Suddenly I was three hundred miles from the expressway. I was in a canoe with my son and a Maine guide. We were on a border lake fishing for smallmouth bass. Above us a bald eagle circled, while his mate guarded their precious chick. The Canadian wind cleared my nostrils of the city fumes. I could feel the gentle rocking of the canoe, hear the slapping of the clear waters against the side of the canoe. I was there! And it was *my* experience, brought about by an interplay of memory and imagination. Not even commuter horns or city sirens could take that experience from me. And it went quite beyond intellect!

Such an experience is only a small part of what your

mind is capable of doing for you, and the fact that others may not understand this, or insist that intellect is all there is, proves to be a tragedy of no little consequence. The person is far too rich for such a simple comprehension.

And if the physical and mental dimensions are ample, consider the spiritual dimension of the person. Here we truly must be awed. Certainly at times we hesitate even to speak about the spiritual side—afraid, perhaps, that others do not understand, or will refuse to acknowledge, this dimension of our nature.

What do I mean by spiritual?

The spiritual dimension has to do with meaning and mystery. These are the two conditions out of which spiritual matters emerge. Also, the spiritual side has to do with matters which are of extraordinary concern, perhaps of ultimate importance, to the person.

A few years ago my wife was rushed to the hospital with a ruptured appendix. Each time I visited her I was struck by the sounds of a woman across the corridor. Over and over this patient kept crying, "Oh, why me, Lord? Why me?" My wife told me that these groans of agony often continued until long after midnight. The continuous cry made everyone uncomfortable. Visitors became nervous. Some patients closed the doors of their rooms. A few complained. I noticed that some nurses shook their heads and seemed to work harder as the groans increased.

No matter how we perceive this episode, it is an example of a cry for meaning—a cry probably as old as humankind and as ancient as pain and suffering. Out of such cries the person's spiritual dimension is formed, for the will-to-meaning, the strong desire to make sense out of the senseless, is the most characteristic of human phenomena. It is one of the things which make us more than animals or automatons.

The search for meaning implies mystery. Why, indeed, should this woman suffer so? Accident? Chance? A cause-effect chain? Evil? These are only words—illusions of control—which try to diminish what remains essentially mysterious. Mystery too is reality. And the spiritual side of the person somehow always seems to sense that there is more unknown than known. That bit of wisdom generates the will-to-meaning. Mystery begets a search for meaning. The quest is a spiritual process, and out of it slowly emerges the spiritual dimension of the person.

Suffering, of course, is only one way in which our spiritual side may be developed. What we consider to be of special and even of ultimate importance also forms part of the spiritual dimension. Our life concerns are dynamic and related to the Self, and it is not always easy to read another person's geography of meaning. What comes closest to the center of one's Self is perceived as crucial. At times a central concern may be one's family. Later in life it might be one's house or possessions. At other times, what is of ultimate concern may be one's search for meaning, or identity, or integrity, or survival.

Sometimes the immediate and the overt beclouds that which we believe to be of ultimate concern. Especially in crises we may discover an immediate need overriding the long-range project of existence to which we are committed. But behind the immediate we can be sure there remain deeper and more pervasive movements. These silent movements help to define what I mean by the spiritual dimension of the person.

Traditionally, matters of meaning and mystery and ultimate concerns were linked to religion. For many persons this is still true. Their faith is worked out and primarily expressed within the language and community of a specific faith commitment. But with the advent and spread of secular religion it is no longer possible to assume that spiritual questions and needs will find a home in a traditional religious system. We find such needs in every corner of life.

I have only touched on the richness of the dimensions discoverable in personhood. Physical, mental, and spiritual are only names used to try to capture what you and I know and feel about ourselves—intertwined in interesting and fascinating ways. You know it of yourself, and you can be sure this complexity is true of others—the wife or husband you may think is an uncomplicated individual, the policeman directing traffic at the intersection, the secretary who types your letters, the hard-hat foreman who gives you your duties for the day, the woman in the

27

flower shop whose hands always seem to be arranging something.

Achieving a Toleration for Ambiguity

The fact is that for most of us entertaining rich meanings of persons does not come easily at first, because such a stance exposes us to much ambiguity. If persons are so complex and there is present in all such a natural depth, is this not a sure way of leaving us confused and baffled? Is it not true that the appreciation of the many dimensions of the person only entangles us in a web of ambiguity?

I really think that the answer is yes. An authentic acknowledgment of the rich meanings implicit in you and me can create a state of ambiguity where events are susceptible to multiple interpretations. This can be painful, causing us to regress to a more simplistic way of viewing ourselves and others.

Psychologists tell us that people differ greatly in their toleration of ambiguity. Some persons seem able to live with ambiguity, and even to find such a state exciting and interest-filled. Others—perhaps most— find ambiguity uncomfortable and require much in the way of mental gymnastics to reduce the am- biguity.

The level and style of your toleration of ambiguity is part of your secret Self. It is just one of the many characteristics which help to make you who you are. And, more important, it is a part of the secret Self which you can come to know better and, if you wish, can change in a way which is in keeping with you as a person.

If you are like many persons I know, your toleration for ambiguity is not especially high. You prefer to change chaos into order, to convert ambiguity into clarity. This, I believe, is a given—something built into our system for survival—and I am not suggesting that you and I need to try to change it in order to hold to rich meanings of persons.

My claim is that the tendency to change ambiguity into clarity *at the expense of the richness of reality* is contrary to building authentic personhood. Because this seems to be such a prevailing and common tendency, I am suggesting that you and I should pay attention to it as part of our psychospiritual project.

How you come to grips with this art of achieving a greater toleration for ambiguity depends a great deal on where you are right now. Perhaps this is not the major problem for you that it has been—and often still is—for me. You may be satisfied that you have a relatively high level of toleration for ambiguity, that you rarely if ever engage in stereotyping or in "premature closure" or in prostrating reality, including the full reality of yourself and others. If this is the case, you can move on to other areas of self-development. But if you sense that your toleration for ambiguity is low, you might wish to turn an inner eye to this tendency.

Of course, you are free to go about this in ways especially appropriate for you. Many ways have been tried by a variety of persons. I can only share with you an approach which has helped me to become aware of how I tend to experience life. It is a simple technique called the Evening Review.[2]

1. At the end of the day, preferably just before going to sleep, find a quiet place free from outside distractions.
2. Close your eyes and concentrate on relaxing your body, quieting your feelings, and as much as possible stilling the activity of your thoughts. Your mind should be quiet and receptive, but *remain alert.*
3. Now review your day in your mind, playing it back like a movie, but backwards. Begin with where you are right now, then recall the dinner hour, and the late afternoon, and so on until morning when you awakened.
4. Throughout the experience it is important to maintain as far as possible the attitude of an objective, detached, noncritical observer, calmly and clearly registering the events of the day,

[2]This particular version was prepared by Steven Kull, Director of Training at the Psychosynthesis Institute, Palo Alto, California, and is reprinted from *Synthesis*, vol. I, no. 1.

neither becoming elated at a success nor becoming depressed and unhappy about a failure. The aim is *not* to relive the experience but to noncritically register in consciousness the *patterns* and *meanings* of the day.

5. Finally, write down your general impressions of what happened and anything special that you have learned.

The Evening Review is a good general format which has helped me gain a greater sense of the whole of life. In using it to get a reading of my toleration for ambiguity, I modify steps 4 and 5 in the following ways: I *do* become a critic by noting each incident in the day when I jumped to generalizations or conclusions which I realize on *honest reflection* did an injustice to an event or another person or to myself. I then write out these instances in my journal, even numbering them to assist me in determining my development in this particular aspect of my life.

As I examine my "track record" over the years, I cannot but conclude that there have been some marked improvements. Although I still catch myself oversimplifying the motives and behavior of myself and my fellow humans, such a tendency is far less evident now than it was several years ago. I have learned to live with the fact that much of life is indeed ambiguous, that I do see through tinted glasses, and this discovery has led me to a new appreciation of the richness of persons.

31

Faith in the Person Process

Holding to rich meanings of persons and achieving greater toleration for ambiguity do carry with them certain dangers. I have found that some persons who eventually agree on the desirability of these qualities of life often enter the process with teeth-grinding and with clenched fists. Such objectives become "goals," pursued with furrowed brow and grim determination. In a later chapter I will say something about the art of waiting. Here, though, I only want to make a claim and to give a testimony about having faith in the person process itself.

By this I mean that there appears to be a certain given about the growth and development of the person, a built-in process that comes with our being human. This is a subtle and fragile point which says in effect that what you are meant to be you will become, and that this process of becoming is integral to your being human. It is subtle and fragile in that there are many factors needed to nurture and promote the development.

As to the nature of this given, I must in all honesty remain mute. I have faith in it because I have experienced it and have watched it move in the lives of others. My guess is that it is something like what Paul was trying to communicate to the Corinthians when he wrote, "I planted, Apollos watered, but God gave the growth" (I Cor. 3:6). In the context of Christian faith, out of which Paul is speaking, *first*

32

God gives the gift, *then* the conditions contribute to the unfolding.

Whether one is Christian or not, the experiential fact appears to be that one does not become a person by striving and straining. Personhood is a gift. And when you own your humanity, the gift becomes yours. It is at the center of you, waiting to become, waiting to move into its fullness. Properly cultivated and given the right environment, it evolves slowly, surely, correctly. This is a faith statement, one which you either accept or do not accept. But make no mistake about it, your decision is important.

2.
Is Life
Problem or Mystery?

Being human, you have undoubtedly formed a general picture of the world which you carry around in your head. Whether it is simple or complex, this general world view is the result of a variety of influences, some obvious, others not so obvious. Some of these influences have their primary roots within; they stem from certain givens, certain forces which are part and parcel of your biological makeup, as well as from your very early experiences.

Psychologists often refer to these aspects as your personality *genotype*. In this term they include a complex assortment of givens—such things as the general activity level and how you tend to react to the world. The genotype also encompasses many motivational tendencies (why you behave as you do) which were established at a very early age. All in all, these many aspects of your personality influence much of what you are and what you can or cannot become. The individual whose genotype includes a set of genetic factors which determines that he will never be over five feet five inches tall will never become a center on a professional basketball team. A woman whose set of genetic factors might destine her to be six feet eight inches tall has very little chance of being a jockey, even with the sports world's reluctant willingness to accept female jockeys!

Many aspects of your personality genotype are much more subtle than the genetic influences on physical height. They might, for example, determine such things as memory, thinking, or learning. Even very early adaptive styles may later determine how well you can delay gratification of certain needs. Your own way of responding to pain, for instance, may be partly the result of forces within the personality genotype.

Of course, the personality genotype is often difficult to know, especially for those of us living in a culture which would have us believe that we can be anything we set our minds to be. This simply is not true, and it is best to acknowledge this aspect of reality.

In my own adventures of the mind and spirit, I have learned that I am not and cannot be an intellectual genius. I am capable of grasping abstract notions only up to a point, and my ability to handle quantitative material (mathematics and statistics, for instance) is not outstanding. Although I have managed to improve in these areas, there is no way that I could become a theoretical mathematician, nor is there any possibility that I could become a statistical consultant in a computer center. No way. Genotypic givens have seen to that.

Perhaps of even greater importance is the realization that I possess some temperamental characteristics which destine me to relate to the world and to other persons primarily in one mode rather than another. For example, I am an introvert, which means that I tend in my relations with the world to move inward rather than outward. I may at times think that it would be nice to be the life of the party, and through considerable effort and strain and conditioning I might even get to the point where I would shake a few more hands and smile a broader smile. But there is no way that I can be an authentic extrovert. There are too many givens for such a radicial change to take place.

What is most miraculous about this, however, is that I can come to own many of these givens. As I shall insist later on, we can even befriend many of them, can sit down with them in a cooperative spirit and make plans together.

Personality, of course, is more than genotype. It is also *phenotype*. The personality phenotype builds on the genotype materials and includes such things as attitudes, values, your preferences and tastes, the roles you play in society, the way you express yourself in interacting with the environment.

In my own self-evaluation, I have discovered that

freedom and honesty have become extremely important for me. I believe I know how they surfaced in my
personality development and what some of the
influences have been in making them especially
important for me. If, now, someone offers me a
position or invites me to join a committee, my
immediate and spontaneous question is, "Will I be free
to express myself, or will I be expected to follow a
party line?" Understand, I might have many other
issues to consider—for example, "What's the pay
like?"—but freedom and honesty consistently push
forward. Undoubtedly, they contribute greatly to how
I tend to see the world, how I see my own and other
people's behavior, how I evaluate the mass of perceptions that come to me every moment of my life. These
two values (only two examples from any number of
possibilities) help to make up my personality
phenotype.

Much of what I see when I observe any other person
is phenotype. In fact, we sometimes tend to think of
another's personality solely in terms of those aspects
or behaviors which belong to the phenotype. But this
is an incomplete picture, and we oversimplify when
we do this.

What I do want to say here is that both the *genotype*
and the *phenotype* aspects—hundreds of factors, in all
kinds of combinations—contribute to your personhood
and to a variety of things which go to make you *you*.
And one of these factors is the general picture of the

world which is uniquely yours, part of the secret or silent Self.

The Problem-Mystery Dilemma

From the variety of dimensions I find in my picture and those of the dozens of persons who have been willing to share their pictures with me, one has come to be exceedingly important to me: *life as problem or as mystery.* It is only one of many dimensions, but I think it is an especially important one.

Before reading on you might reflect on the proposition yourself. How do you understand the question, Is life primarily a problem to be solved or a mystery to be lived? Have you made a decision in regard to this issue? Has a decision been made for you? Or are you at a place in life where the question is coming to you for the first time?

For most of my life, I considered life primarily as a problem to be solved. I don't believe I thought about this in any systematic way. It was more like an unconscious mood, something that had set in like the beginning of the hornets' nest under the sundeck of my house. I didn't see exactly when that got started either; and even after I first noticed the gray bump under the sundeck, I forgot about it and pretty much left it alone. It was only when it got to be the size of a football and its many residents began to crisscross close to my nose that I really noticed the nest and began to think that I ought to do something about it.

Psychologically speaking, a lot of reflection was required before I was able to shift in emphasis from problem to mystery. It was not simply a matter of making a decision. This was something that had to be lived out in life, to be thought through and felt through in a gentle fashion. Nor was it necessary to destroy one possibility in order to embrace another. Rather, the process was one of becoming *aware* of the second possibility, of seriously entertaining it as another guiding question capable of giving direction to life.

Why should the issue of problem *vs.* mystery wait so long to surface? What determines when, or even if, the question seeps into consciousness?

Conditions Which Surface the Question

My personal conviction is that transitions in life often provide the context in which the problem-mystery question is raised. I think especially of all those many periods in life when we appear to be moving from one point to another and have some awareness that this is happening. These transitions may be dramatic and conspicuous, as when a person decides to commit his or her life as a religious, or when parents sense what the coming of a first child means to them, or when one loses a loved one and must adjust to the fact that one must live from now on without that person, or when one's death is very close at hand and must be faced. At times transitions may be less conspicuous, at least from an external viewpoint, as when a twelve-year-old becomes a teen-ager, or when a promotion comes to a person who may not be certain of his or her ability to handle the new responsibilities, or when a religious person's faith seems to be losing its luster.

Some transitions are judged as undramatic by others, but the fact is that from the inner perspective any experience of transition may be dramatic, even traumatic. The "quiet desperation" which Thoreau tells us about can be, and often is, a sign of serious transition not made public. The secret Self may be in the very midst of a transitional process, yet no such change appears evident to others. Conspicuous and inconspicuous transitions can be both painful and pleasant and can take place at such depths that they hardly disturb surface waters. Really, we should learn to walk gently when it comes to appraising the transitions of others and of ourselves.

Although there are many kinds of transitions which originate in a variety of contexts and depend on the personal history of the individual, there is a commonality too, a range of transitions that all of us can anticipate. Many of these may be called developmental, since they are related to the simple fact that we become older as we live. An example is the transition generated by the realization that we are entering the second half of life.

We often joke about this transitional phase of life with such phrases as "the dangerous forties" or "the seven-year itch" or "the middle-age syndrome." Humor may help and can be one way of tolerating the inevitable, but too often humor alone falls into a form of denial which prevents us from turning the bland developmental fact into a productive opportunity for authentic growth.

Some psychologists observe that the first half of life is spent in struggling with the problems of status and survival. We must get an education. We must earn a living. We must learn to relate to others in ways which contribute to our survival. These and many other activities come to preoccupy us. At times these coping activities may sap all our energies, and we actually begin to believe that this *is* life, this is all there is. Life is coping, scratching for a living, struggling to make ends meet, groaning after a secure place in the sun, doing a job. And all this means that life is one great problem, and we are essentially problem-solvers.

But you and I have another side, and that other side will let itself be known sooner or later. In a sense, this other side says, "Look, there's more to life than solving problems and achieving goals. There's a *quality* to life, and I want you to meet it." This "voice" may come to us in a variety of ways, depending on our conditions in life and our individual personalities, including those genotypic and phenotypic characteristics noted above.

41

As I write these words, I can dimly hear five men singing a Mass on the other side of the farmhouse in which I am staying. They have come to live in this house for forty days and forty nights, devoting their time to prayer, contemplation, and a simple life-style. Although these men are monks who ordinarily live in monasteries, they too have heard a cry from another side of themselves. As monks they got caught up in a round of activities and apostolates which bumped them around and dulled their spirits. They are here not simply to retreat from these ego activities, but to recapture and live the mystery behind their calling. They would be the first to admit that their way is not the only way, but I think they would all agree that there are times when every person must field the question, Is life essentially a problem to be solved or a mystery to be lived?

For many of us, the question is not put the way a professional religious might hear it. It may come to us through a discontentment or a boredom which seems to run through our whole body. The words may be in a language we don't even understand, as in the case of the busy industrialist with the constant headaches whose muscles and stomach are asking him the question.

Although the question may surface in many ways and in many forms, once it taps your consciousness it is a call difficult to ignore. You are being asked to respond, to make some sort of decision, to come to own

42

the question and your answer in a style which is peculiarly yours.

Consequences of Denying or Accepting the Mystery Answer

I would not presume to tell you what denying the answer that life is a mystery to be lived will mean for you. The consequences will depend on many of the genotypic and phenotypic characteristics which are yours and yours alone. I can only speak for myself and in terms of illustrations which have come from other lives willingly shared with me. The evidence is based on a relatively narrow range of experiences, and they are shared with you not as "ultimate truths" or even wise maxims. They are simply generalizations arising out of a sample of lived experiences.

First, I believe that if you deny the mystery answer—or if you fail even to recognize it—you are destined to exist in a crucible of coping. What does this mean? It may mean a variety of things, not the least of which could be a certain tenseness about life in general.

In my own case, whenever I feel myself slipping back into a problem orientation I begin to see my daily contacts and experiences as essentially issues which must be used or surmounted. I begin to think about those I counsel in terms of what I might *do* to *make*

43

them see what they might *do* to rid themselves of their "hang-ups." And, too, I am inclined to evaluate my day-by-day experiences in a fashion which leads me to feel tense and even anxious. I find, for example, that when I slip back into seeing life as problem my personal journal reflects many complaints and gripes and even my recorded dreams tend to be dreams of conflict and puzzlement.

A client of mine once said, "I swear I think I was born to be unhappy." Sally had a long history of negative events—a bad marriage, a brother who had committed suicide, unhappiness in her work, and so forth. Life had become a series of crises, and she had come to expect them; one was waiting for her "just around the corner." Even the smallest decision—like renting a new apartment—became a great problem preoccupying her mind for months. At times her tense expectations actually penetrated her physical being in the form of headaches and a weariness far too intense for her years.

We talked about the reality of her life for many hours. I helped her learn to relax and to enjoy some of the gifts that came to her—gifts which she had not really earned: the bunch of daisies her little daughter brought to her one Sunday morning, the gas station attendant's kindness toward her when she was having troubles with her old car, the half-acre of land inherited from an aunt and now the place where she could put her mobile home, the fact that her daughter is intelligent and beautiful. We soon discovered that she was indeed the recipient of many good things and that most of these had come to her while she was simply waiting. This was not an "accentuate the positive, eliminate the negative" sort of exercise. We were exploring reality together and beginning to sense the nature of grace and to appreciate how taking it easy can also yield up to us a whole range of basically good experiences. Part of this "taking it easy" condition, at least for Sally, meant learning to relax and permit life to play with her a bit and to abandon her traditional stance of tenseness and her problem-solving tendencies.

A second consequence seemingly implicit in the problem-mystery dilemma has to do with the value we assign to quiet and subtle realities. I believe that in a problem-solving stance we tend to perceive only the grossest sort of realities, the mass movements around us, the most common and general conditions in the world. I have found that part of the mystery side of the dilemma alerts me to the more subtle, yet exciting, aspects of the world. This was part of what Sally began to sense when she became more relaxed.

Some years ago when I was in the midst of struggling through the problem-mystery issue, I decided to slip away from my preoccupation with work by developing a hobby. I chose photography. At first I found it exceedingly difficult to participate in my new hobby for its own sake—or for my own sake. Instead, I felt compelled to master techniques and even to consider the ways in which my new hobby might be made to pay off. Where might I sell my pictures? How much equipment would I need to take the kind of professional photographs accepted by magazines? I soon found myself thinking of my hobby as a series of problems to be solved, a sequence of self-training hurdles I had to clear before I could really enjoy my avocation.

Then one day while I was sitting on a bench looking out across the snow-covered campus an impression came to me in an unusual fashion. I had completed my undergraduate work in this same college and had lived near it and worked in it for nearly a decade—but suddenly I saw it for the first time!

There it was—quiet mounds of white snow crowning rustic bricks, a sundial's dark shadow breaking across a bench, the irregular pattern of a forsythia bush's shadow on the snow, the roughness of cement walls cracked a hundred times by frozen water, the gnarled branches of oaks coming to the end of a long life. Suddenly I realized how my photography was making me more aware of shadow and texture. Now I was seeing the marvelous patterns resulting from the interplay of light and darkness.

Here was a new world where delicate realities were waiting to be perceived. *This* was the grace of my new hobby—the rewards of an enlightened perception. All I had to do was let them in, become a part of the fullness of a reality which had been there all the time.

My contention is that accepting life as mystery gives new meanings to the quiet realities of life, and that this is not only good but better than the tightness of a problem-centered existence. At least, this seems true to me at this point in my own development.

A third result of seeing life essentially as a mystery to be lived rather than as a problem to be solved is that such a view tends to bring into serious question the tendency to strain after fullness, to fret and groan over some ideal we may have about how we ought to be. Often, in working with individuals seeking greater spiritual development, I find it helpful to get some general idea of the person's image of maturity or what he or she would like to become. Once this image is fairly well established, we spend some time talking about the manner of moving to this different level of being. And it is here that I believe the problem-mystery issue may help to determine the mode we accept as being most productive.

If we are basically problem-oriented, we tend to want to achieve the image through a process of conscious straining. We grit our teeth, furrow our brow, and strain after the image with determination. We see greater maturity resting at some point far ahead, and between it and where we now stand are many barriers to be overcome. The big problem is to achieve the new vision, but before that can be accomplished we need to solve a whole row of mini-problems.

What's wrong with this view? Is it a natural and logical way to proceed?

I cannot argue against such a procedure in general

47

terms. It may well be that you have achieved many new levels of awareness in this fashion. I can only note that when life is viewed as a mystery to be lived another possibility comes into being. This way has far more to do with waiting and with patience than it does with straining after a new level of being.

Part of this has to do with a rather simple psychological principle: we do not usually achieve the desired state by going at it directly. The person who strains after happiness rarely finds it. The person who is determined to be mature hardly ever is. It seems that we need to look off target in order to hit the bull's-eye.

I remember Edith, a girl who wanted more than anything in the world to be attractive and liked. In talking about her ideal image, Edith at one point even sketched a portrait of how she wanted to be. The girl in the picture was blonde with "bedroom eyes." She was tall and had an attractive figure. Edith had her ideal sitting in a red sports car with several handsome men gathered about in conversation. We talked about the picture for a long time, drawing in details and adding meaningful colors to give even greater vividness.

Finally I said, "Okay, Edith, now let's put the picture away for a while and deal with some pretty specific things."

For some months we talked about a wide range of concerns, but mostly about Edith's opinion of herself. We covered her childhood, her fears, her delights, her

IS LIFE PROBLEM OR MYSTERY?

relationships with her parents and brothers and sisters, and especially her thoughts and feelings about her relationship with me. Many months after we had begun our conversations, I said to Edith one day "I like you, Edith. You're a very attractive person, and I actually look forward to our hour together."

Our relationship was such that these words were said easily and without embarrassment. Edith knew that I meant what I said, and she could accept the words without apology or stammering.

A few weeks later she said, "I've never felt quite so good about myself. I like me and I find others do, too. I'm even beginning to tolerate my many shortcomings."

Then we took Edith's ideal portrait out of the desk drawer and had a good laugh together, for although Edith was indeed more attractive now, she was still a brunette, a bit flat-chested, and she drove a VW, not a red sports car! Still, she had succeeded in moving to another level of being.

Perhaps Edith could have done this more directly, and in a more intense way—perhaps even consciously trying to emulate her ideal image. And perhaps that might have worked. I don't think so, and neither does Edith. Our way had involved some pain and some struggle, but it was far more a process of befriending what Edith already was, of letting things happen in a context of concern and care, of permitting mystery to have its way with her at least for this period of transition.

49

The Subtle Art of Balancing

It is quite apparent in what I am writing here that I am coming down hard on the mystery part of this life view. It is now necessary to qualify some of my bias a little in regard to this answer. I stress the life-as-mystery angle because I am convinced that most of us in the Western world, and especially those of us reared in an achievement-oriented culture, are conditioned to view life as a problem to be solved. Much of what is presented to us as children, adolescents, and adults is couched in the problem-solving mode. And, as I have noted already, a great part of the first half of life is geared to problem-solving, often out of sheer necessity.

The problem-solving side of our nature gets developed almost automatically in our culture, including our major institutions. This is so true, I am arguing, that we may actually come to believe that this way of looking at life is all there is: we are indeed essentially problem-solvers and that ends the matter.

I suggest that this is not only untrue but is a dangerous untruth, both for the individual as a person and for the world at large. I have hit hard at this point.

But equally it is true that life as problem to be solved yields some fine accomplishments. I do not wish to say that life as problem is wrong and that life as mystery is right. Both views are realities—realities which the Self must manage and befriend. In the long run, the call is to discover a dynamic balance between these two orientations, to search for a relationship which gives integrity to both, and which, in time, will yield up a form of authentic personhood. This is the project we face as human beings.

3.
The Art of Waiting

If you are anything like I am, you tend to go after a goal with vigor and zeal. You may be one of those persons who believe that struggle and concentration are prerequisites for accomplishment, and, frankly, I am not going to try to argue against such a stance or to claim that determination is fruitless in the attempt to achieve an objective. I have no doubt that concentration and training are necessary attributes in many areas of achievement.

My main purpose in this chapter is to suggest that when it comes to the psychospiritual project, another approach might prove far more appropriate. At least, I have found—as have some others I have known—that another mode is available to you and to me which could prove to be an especially good one to utilize in coming to appreciate the reality of the secret Self.

The Tendency to Struggle for Maturity

The tendency to struggle for greater maturity is not to be seen in a negative way. Its presence is motivational. If we did not have such a tendency, we might never advance much in the areas of psychological and spiritual growth. Indeed, there appears to be a natural inertia when it comes to these areas of growth. Perhaps one of the most difficult tendencies the psychotherapist, counselor, or spiritual director faces in trying to help people grow is resistance, which may be conscious or unconscious. When it is conscious, the client or patient simply withholds information from the counselor. There may be a variety of reasons for this—fear, shame, distrust, for example—but whatever the reason, the client is refusing to grow. When resistance is unconscious—that is, the client is not aware of what he or she is doing—it is often quite passive and seemingly innocent. Perhaps the client misses an appointment. Or maybe he or she carefully avoids talking about those areas most crucial to psychic health—always for "very good and logical reasons."

This tendency to resist growth and insight varies greatly among individuals. It is a difficult tendency to identify because it is often very quiet and subtle.

My hunch is that the greater our resistance to growth and change experiences, the greater the intensity of our struggle toward maturity *once we have performed the act of will necessary to commit ourselves to a project of development.*

I think in this regard of a young priest I met some years ago. Let's call him Father Sebastian. He was an especially brilliant man with a fine academic history and a brief but excellent record of apostolates. Vaguely dissatisfied with his formal intellectual achievements, he decided to take a few university courses before asking for a leave which would enable him to study for an M.A. degree. Because he was late in registering and could not get into his first preference, he found himself taking a course in group dynamics. What a strange situation for Father Sebastian!

During the first week he found the course impossible. After five sessions, he did not have one page of notes in his notebook! There was no extensive bibliography, and the instructor rarely lectured. The young priest was at a loss. Even when he attempted to contribute to the seminar discussion, he was disappointed in the responses he got from other class members. One of them even said, "Lord, Father, we don't need your head trip. I know you're bright and so does everyone else—so let's knock off the head trip."

This drove Father Sebastian into an angry silence. He decided he would ride out the brief summer course without saying another word.

About the fourth week, while Father Sebastian was having coffee in the university cafeteria, the instructor of the group dynamics course joined him at his table.

The instructor talked mostly about some theoretical matters and shared with the priest a book he was reading entitled *Our Many Selves,* by Elizabeth O'Connor. "Take it along," he said. "You might like it."

If there was one thing Father Sebastian could do well it was read books, and he read *Our Many Selves* over the weekend. It thrilled him. The idea that we are many selves, not one, fascinated the young priest as nothing had done before. At the very next class meeting, he found a chance to talk about the book and gave a comprehensive review of it. When he finished, there was a long silence. Finally, one of the other participants asked, "So how many of your selves do you know?"

Father Sebastian was struck dumb by the question. He knew by now that there were many selves that made up Father Sebastian, but he knew too that he was intimately aware of only a few. That evening at prayers the young priest, by an act of will, decided that he would ask for a year's leave, not to get another academic degree but to go looking for the selves he had so carefully avoided.

It was several months later that I met Father Sebastian. He was not wearing a clerical collar, his hair was quite long, and he had the beginnings of a beard. He was contemplating leaving his order; he might even get married. He was participating in workshops just about every weekend—Gestalt, trans-actional analysis, and so on. He wasn't certain what he wanted, but he was sure that religious life was far too constricting. He was free at last!

After about six conversations, however, Father Sebastian began to weep. "No, I am not free," he confessed. "These many activities have a hold on me. I feel compelled to participate in every workshop that comes along—and each one seems like a savior. But then it fades, and I'm off to another group. I've found that there are many selves to me, but they're all going in different directions. And frankly, I'm weary."

It took some time for this young priest to realize that his struggling after greater maturity was really only driving him to frantic distraction. His resistance to growth had been so strong and pervasive that, once it was overcome, the new project had flooded in upon him with a violence he could not control—a violence which was now controlling him. Father Sebastian needed to learn something about how to wait.

The Waiting Principle

Many years ago a young Frenchwoman named Simone Weil wrote some words about the way God comes and goes which have always seemed to me to be especially apt as a description of the waiting principle. Even for those of you who dislike "God talk," the picture she paints may be helpful:

Over the infinity of space and time, the infinitely more infinite love of God comes to possess us. He comes at his own time. We have the power to consent to receive him or to

56

refuse. If we remain deaf, he comes back again and again like a beggar, but also, like a beggar, one day he stops coming. If we consent, God puts a little seed in us and he goes away again. From that moment God has no more to do; neither have we, except to wait.[1]

I have spent many hours meditating on this passage. Although it speaks of the ways of God, I believe it is also a way of coming to know the secret Self. As I noted in the introduction, it is often during periods of transition that the opportunities for growth become especially evident to us. At these crucial points, we are free to say *yes* or *no*. The saying of *yes*—the *yes* project, if you will—is itself important because it is the planting of a seed that symbolizes the willingness to explore the Self in greater detail and depth. The saying of *no* is equally important because, if said often enough, it determines that the secret Self shall remain secret, not only to others but to ourselves as well. We die then, spiritually, although life may continue on and on and on . . .

Perhaps, though, what is important about the *yes* response is that it is a beginning requiring a certain kind of waiting. When speaking of God's actions, Simone Weil says that once God has planted the seed, he goes away. He has no more to do. But then she adds the perplexing phrase "neither have we, except to wait."

It took me many years to reach the point where I

[1]*Waiting for God*, trans. Emma Craufurd (New York: G. P. Putnam's Sons, 1951), p. 69.

could accept this seemingly passive attitude, either in relation to God's nature or in relation to the evolution of the Self. Part of this resistance is due to seeing life as a problem to be solved. But even after one has consented to the legitimacy of the mystery stance, it is still difficult to integrate the waiting principle into the project of self-discovery and growth.

I think part of the willingness to take the waiting principle seriously rests in the *yes/no* decision. An authentic *yes* makes waiting possible. Indeed, implicit in the *yes* seed is a slow, gentle, and even tender process of evolution, far removed from the strain and struggle of the alternative. However, when we say *yes* tongue-in-cheek, as I think we often do, the waiting principle is not really a viable mode for us, and we find many excellent reasons for electing a more active principle of growth.

I am reminded here of the fisherman who seems to have infinite patience, who is able to fish from dawn until midnight and not catch a single fish. "You might as well fish in a bathtub," the less patient person will say. But the patient fisherman *knows* that such a criticism is invalid. For at some point he has seen signs of fish in this lake—he has said *yes*—and he senses from experience that with patience he will catch a fish. True, the good fisherman will change lures, cast to different depths, retrieve at various speeds, and so on, in order to catch his quarry. But he carries out all these little maneuvers with quiet patience, knowing that in the final analysis the quarry must still come to him. If he learns to wait well and in the spirit of the quest, things will happen.

Although the illustration is an oversimplification of my conviction that the waiting principle is integral to discovery of the secret Self, it does, I think, reflect a genuine pattern inherent in the nature of the Self. More literary and picturesque is the old Chinese saying: "The way of the sage is to act without striving."

The Natural Development of the Self

I believe that once you say *yes* in the midst of transitions, the seed of self-realization is planted and a wise sort of waiting is all that is required of you. Your task is to find ways of permitting the seed to germinate and flower. But for most of us wise waiting is not easy. We learn to cooperate with the natural development of the Self—if we learn at all—at different times and in different ways.

Still, you must wonder, are there not some guidelines, perhaps at least a chart with markings of depths, shoals, and reefs?

As one who is thoroughly convinced that meeting the secret Self is basically a solitary process with amazing peculiarities implicit in it, I hesitate to outline any sort of natural development of the Self. Up until recently I thought that awareness of the Self was something that could be related to the usual phases defined by developmental psychology—those general steps you often see discussed in introductory textbooks. At least, I was convinced that the discovery, or rediscovery, of the Self could not take place until the first half of life was over. Although I still feel that the twilight years tend to be especially suited for the rediscovery of the Self, I am no longer convinced that the process can only take place then. In fact, I think that such an idea can be dangerous and could well lead to a form of spiritual abortion. Believing that one can best learn to befriend the Self during the second half of life might lead someone to postpone a process vital to his or her full development.

Several weeks ago I had the opportunity of being in a growth group in which there was a seventeen-year-old girl. At first I was a bit perturbed, feeling that her immaturity would be a limiting factor in our conversations. It soon became apparent, however, that when it came to addressing questions of the spirit—especially those deeper issues of meanings and values—her words and expressions were on target and close to the feeling level. As she shared areas of her secret Self I felt them to be akin to mine. Over thirty years separated us, but at center we were alike in many respects.

Although chronology and the experiences which accompany normal development are not unimportant, I do not believe we can understand the development of the Self strictly along those lines. I am driven instead to draw on the following analogy.

Some months ago I was shown a small wooden lamp shaped like a lotus flower. In the center is a light, and surrounding it are the petals. When the petals are closed, no light is visible; but by turning the knob one can permit the petals to open and the center to cast its brightness in all directions. The wider the petals are opened, the more light escapes.

Although I had long known the symbolic meaning of the lotus flower in the mystical tradition of the East, I had never quite related it to the evolution of the Self in the peculiar and startling way which came to me on this occasion. Perhaps being a part of the technological age had sensitized me more to the little electrical lamp than to the natural flower itself, but whatever the reason, the lotus lamp struck me as being an unusually appropriate illustration of the natural development of the Self.

The little knob could be thought of as the will, that crucial part of you and me which makes us human and which partly accounts for decisions and intentions. Without it one would be little more than a buffeted-about dot in the universe, completely at the mercy of environmental turbulence. You may be inclined to argue about it or to explore the great philosophical debates which have centered on the subject—but once you have experienced the will, you tend to find such arguments interesting but hardly relevant to its use in the way to self-realization.

Saying *yes* to the process of self-realization is one way of turning the knob that lets the petals begin to unfold. That one expression of the will allows a splinter of light to escape, and you can literally feel its warmth. This first awareness of the actual brilliance of the secret Self is an experience of great meaning. You feel the power and warmth of the center, and it is at first a good feeling.

But the splinter of light may bring with it some fears as well. With that initial *yes* you may pick up another set of feelings, some quite negative. For there is risk here. After all, keeping the petals tightly closed may give you a feeling of security. Learning to live with the process of spiritual growth brings with it certain implications for our relationships and our day-by-day doings. Still, the petals are there; and we cannot help being challenged by the light at the center of the lamp if we are at all sensitive to the need to grow.

What is often disturbing is that the development of the secret Self is not uniform or neatly predictable. In one sense, the petals do not open smoothly and steadily. More often than not, development is erratic, at times discouragingly slow. And then, just when we begin to note the gentle unfolding, the petals may close again. Some travelers have called this point "the dark night of the soul."

Most of us have come to assume that a "natural development" ought to be steady and certain, completely predictable. Perhaps we come by this idea quite honestly through our general perceptions of changes in nature, including the seasons of the year. But I believe we make such an assumption mostly out of need, not out of careful observation. My hunch is that a great deal of development in nature is slow and faltering, at times even erratic and surprising.

Whether or not this is true in nature, it does seem true in the development of the Self. It may be that our use of analogy with nature is itself faulty and that we should simply observe the ways of the spirit and not assume that they will copy natural processes. For from what I have seen in myself, and from what I have been able to observe in others, we err if we assume that the development of the Self is smooth, predictable, and certain in its expression.

Learning to Live with the Process of Spiritual Growth

Here I wish to raise up two factors which can, and frequently do, maim or even destroy the principle of waiting: what others think and our own discouragement.

No person is an island. You and I move in a complex of interpersonal relationships. I depend on you, you depend on me, even in the communication of meaning in these written words. Although I sit alone at my desk as I write this, I am trying to relate to you. I try to imagine what you are like. I want to know you; and I hope you want to know me.

Despite what critics have said about the egocentricity of those persons devoted to the development of the secret Self, most spiritual travelers are acutely aware of the social nature of their project. They value the influence of others. They are not naïve about the power of others, including the power and influences of society and culture.

But in the spiritual process there is a point, however infinitesimal, where we each stand alone. There is a solitariness about the development of the secret Self which is real and authentic, a centerpoint where decisions must be made solely in terms of one's own spiritual qualities. At this point, standing in the eye of the hurricane, *you are you and the voice must be yours*.

This is not an easy truth to ground in our day-to-day life, because it usually involves us in conflicts with others, especially with persons who have not said *yes* to the project of spiritual growth. Often these persons are well-meaning. At times they are genuinely concerned over our welfare; and they truthfully see the search for the secret Self as irrelevant, perhaps even frightening.

Because we respect them, perhaps even love them, we are pulled toward their opinions like metal filings to a magnet. Can I be right when so many say that I am wrong? Can this spiritual process be important when such a respected crowd tells me it is unimportant? Is there a chance that I have been caught in an illusion, a fog of vaporized nonsense, as some are claiming? Can it be that my commitment to discover the secret Self is only a sign of an inner weakness, as a few of my friends imply?

What others say of our spiritual sojourn is important; but we must resist with quiet persistence any and all attempts to abort this transition period. We are called upon to live with the almost inevitable fact that not all our friends and relatives will be able to share in our spiritual challenge. Once the *yes* has come forth from us, this social factor will need to be accepted as an inevitable consequence, but one which need not lead to defeat in our attempts to let the waiting principle have its way.

The second inevitable consequence implicit in the process of waiting is discouragement. Here an act of will is essential, for, as I have said already, the natural development of the Self is often erratic and unpredictable. Because the process is long and characterized by ups and downs, it is quite easy to become discouraged. What makes this discouragement especially powerful and destructive is that support is usually not close at hand.

In many difficult activities of life we have the support of family and community, and these prove to be a resource to stave off crippling discouragement. But spiritual development is frequently seen in quite a different way by those who have not said *yes* to the growth process. One may be driven into a certain kind of loneliness with very few weapons to ward off the dark dynamic of discouragement.

At such times we must turn to the very source of the process for our strength. The spiritual quest holds the qualities we need. This is the faith we must have if discouragement is to be transformed into a positive force.

For some it is essential at this time to have a guide, a person who can be trusted and who has experienced the loneliness and discouragement which are implicit in the development of the spiritual life. Sometimes a book can help; or our own meditations and prayers can keep us moving, if these modes have become part of our project. But for most of us it seems essential to know that at least one other (for some, One Other) is there offering us guidance and support. Then it is that the negative readings from others and the inner dynamic of discouragement can be faced and even, perhaps, befriended.

4.
Living with Time

Contemporary psychologists and anthropologists have made some interesting and astute observations about the variety of ways people orient themselves to the world in terms of time. In this chapter I wish to relate some of this material to the project of self-discovery. I want to share a few of my own ideas about time and how you and I can own it in a way which will help us on our journey inward. And I hope to be able to show that *presence* is a key condition for the discovery of the secret Self. But first it is necessary to say a few words about finding out where you are at this moment.

Perhaps the greatest danger you and I face in starting on the adventure of self-discovery and -realization is the bag of habits we carry around with us. Not that this assortment of habits is necessarily bad;

but there is a very good chance that your habit repertoire has evolved and developed with physical and social survival in mind. Many of our habitual ways, including those special mind-sets that we have come to take for granted, have attached themselves to us out of sheer necessity. If they have helped us in our adjustment, we hold them to our bosoms with an eagerness that tends to make them part of ourselves. And it is only natural that in considering another project of existence—the essentially psychospiritual one of self-discovery—we should draw on those habits already made part of our everyday tasks of responding and surviving in the world.

Here I wish to consider those habits that relate us to the world in terms of time. And because I really believe that time—at least our experience of it—can be a major distraction in the process of self-realization, I am going to write about past, present, and future in a way that may at first seem somewhat negative. But, as I hope to demonstrate, these time dimensions, when truly owned by us, can be helpful companions on the journey to discovery of the secret Self.

The Tyranny of the Past

Many people who come for counseling begin by talking about the past—their past. Memory seems to dominate their account of life. Even when they are encouraged to talk about plans for the future or to share their intentions, it is not long before they drift back into the past. And for good reason. The past is easily available, escapes our sense of responsibility and will, and tends to be that part of our awareness which is, after all, finished and fixed. Much of it is now safe, holding no possibilities for us anymore. Or so it seems.

In the psychospiritual project, the past can be helpful. What I remember often reveals what I value. I find in my own counseling that if a person is given an opportunity to let an image come into his or her mind, it is frequently an image dredged up from the past. And more often than not, this image tells much about the present and may even contain some important hints about the person's destiny.

I was recently asked by my guide to relax and permit an image to come into my mind. The image that came was one from my past: I saw myself as a high school freshman standing with a group of boys, all eager to make the football team and knowing that not all of us would be selected. In the middle of the gymnasium floor was a pile of equipment and uniforms, the leftovers after the coach had selected his first and second teams. Now that same coach walked in front of us, the scrubs, looking us up and down, judging our size, posture, and so on. When he pointed at one and grunted, "You!" the teen-ager went scurrying to the pile of equipment, trying desperately to find sweaters and pads that came close to fitting. And there I stood—all 110 pounds of me—waiting, waiting . . .

As the image took on greater and greater clarity, so too did the feelings that had stormed through my body: hurt, fear, anger, expectation, frustration, sadness, and humiliation. And every emotion had been carefully hidden from the coach.

That image from the past caught me in its force, and I realized that I had been trying to be what I was not meant to be. I had placed supreme value on something which really ought not to have been valued so highly. There I was, shamefully tense, waiting to be selected and being rejected by a relatively insensitive authority figure.

What lessons can we discover in images like this born out of memory? That particular one brought me a dozen lessons, each one telling me just a bit more of my secret Self and the ways I had learned to deny it, to hide it from others and, worse, from my own awareness.

You have such images waiting to be viewed in the light of the *yes* project which leads to the opening of the petals of the secret Self. And in this sense, the past needs to be befriended, to be brought gently into consciousness and recognized as an important factor in the search for self-realization.

That, however, is the major extent of its value in the project of self-realization. The past can be helpful, even necessary—but it is crippling as well. And too often we are lulled into an unproductive preoccupation with it.

This is especially true if, in contemplating your past, you find a series of failures or limitations. "What is the use?" you may ask. "My memory shows only disappointment and defeat. There is little there which gives promises of a Self worthy of attention." Such arguments may be very real, rooted in actual experiences, but these negative memories are only reflections of a period in time when the secret Self was not known, perhaps hardly imagined. They are events, real or imagined, which were created and interpreted by false selves or by a dim consciousness of the Self.

This sort of past can act as a mean judge who communicates only negative images. It is not unusual for a person interested in greater self-discovery to become encapsulated by the past. It can happen to you, especially as you discover how easy it really is to dredge up past events. With just a little practice and encouragement, you may find that your past holds a wide assortment of memories, some of which can easily be related to your most troublesome problems of the moment. You might even claim that, given your particular past, there doesn't seem to be much hope for a bright future. Indeed, some inward travelers have concluded that their past *is* their destiny; and such a conclusion has led them to abandon the search for the secret Self. When this happens, the past has become a tyrant, chaining us to a false evaluation of itself.

You owe it to yourself to reflect on the past now that

71

you have said *yes* to the project of discovering the secret Self. If the *yes* has an authentic ring, you will soon discover that the past *is* important; but not all-important. The past *does* determine your destiny, but not all of your destiny. It *can* tell you a great deal about yourself, but it has neither the power nor the full measure of time necessary to comprehend your total Self. The past, in other words, can come under your influence. You can own it. You can use it. You can befriend it.

The Tyranny of Tomorrow

If the past can hold you captive and keep you from accepting the secret Self in its fullness, a preoccupation with the future can be just as crippling. In our time, the word *futuristics* has come into its own. There are even professional futurists, with clubs and organizations to support them. And most of us have a genuine interest in potentialities, in what might be.

Again, our roles as persons ready to take seriously the personal journey should cause us to appreciate the importance of an orientation toward the future. Projections of what might be *do* help to determine what will be. If, for instance, I see myself in the future as a more sensitive person, open to wider perceptions and relating to others in a more genuine way, such projections will have an influence on what I become.

It is not so much the future itself which furnishes the motivation for growth and development, as it is *our perceptions of the future*. If, indeed, I have pessimistic visions of the future, thinking it to be filled with failure and disappointment, those visions will condition the process of becoming. It is true, of course, that reality—so important in self-realization—may alter, perhaps even reverse, my projections; nevertheless, the vision remains influential in my psychic development.

Under no circumstances would I want to suggest that being oriented to the time dimension we call future is in itself contrary to the full realization of the secret Self. Like the past, the future can assist you and me as we step into the process of self-discovery. The tyranny of tomorrow is active, however, whenever the future pulls us ahead, yanking our feet from the present.

At an experiential level we can sense this without any reference to the great philosophical debates over the nature of time. You can, with the help of some self-reflection, get the *feel* of this tyranny of the future, as I did recently in a conversation with a fellow psychologist. We were having lunch together to talk about a mutual interest. After about fifteen minutes of conversation, my friend stopped in the middle of a sentence and said, "Wait a minute, I am not present; and I don't think you are either. We're talking to one another, but we're not here."

He was right, and there followed a period of

confession. He admitted that his mind was cluttered with thoughts of a paper he was writing to be delivered some weeks later. And I admitted that I was thinking of a committee meeting immediately following lunch, a meeting I felt might be quite emotional and confrontational.

Both of us had become victims of the future, which had quietly, ruthlessly, jerked us away from one another. We had let the future take us away. We were no longer present to one another.

Since I believe that the discovery of the secret Self is essentially a *now* process, I am especially sensitive to the tyranny of the future. In my own life, I have found this dimension of time to be even more ruthless than the past. It is often so insidious that its tyranny is hardly noticed. Many times it has held me in its grasp, and I did not know it until too late; an opportunity for presence had been lost, a chance for personal growth had been aborted.

This disruption in our psychological and spiritual development can be partially avoided by the full utilization of the present.

The Creative Now

What does it mean to be focused in the present?

This can best be described through examples. When my colleague and I were conversing but thinking about events in the future, we were not participating in the now. Nor were we present to one another. He could feel it, and I could feel it.

Perhaps at this very moment you should pause and ask yourself, "Am I with these words I am reading? Is what this writer trying to tell me alive in the present?" Try it. Test whether you are *with me* as you read these words.

Whatever your individual response to this little experiment, you must at times have felt that psychologically you were not wholly or even mostly in the present. Frequently memories are pushing against you from behind, and plans are trying to invade you from up front. And although this is a condition you cannot consistently avoid, you can keep from being invaded by past and future and prevent these modes from exercising a tyranny over you. This, I maintain, is what must be done in the project of self-discovery and -realization.

The now dimension is where creativity finds its home. The present moment is really the heart of discovery, and it is where both past and future are transformed so as to have meaning for self-discovery. And although it is true that on your journey toward the secret Self you will find yourself shifting attention from past to future, your primary task is to discover how to balance past and future concerns in the service of the present.

Perhaps the little drawing on page 76 will help you understand this better. The baseline represents time in the outside world—Past, Present, and Future clearly marked. The wheel on the "track of time" is the individual, who also has a past and a present and a future. If the wheel simply turns, the individual's past, present, and future touch the base in an on-and-off manner, in a clickety-click sort of relationship—which is indeed the way most of us live the greater part of our lives.

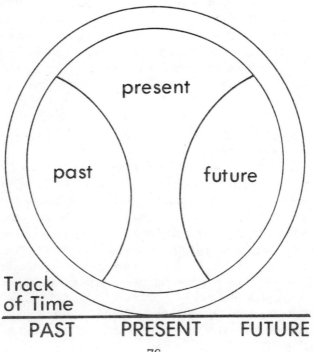

In the drawing, however, the distribution of time dimensions is "frozen" as it ought to be in the process of discovering the secret Self. Imagine the wheel continuing down the track—since life goes on even when we are engaged in psychological and spiritual development—with the inner divisions remaining as pictured. The now or present segment of the individual is in touch with the track, and the past and future segments come into contact with the track through the present. Past and future are not eliminated, but make contact via the present.

You may wonder why I stress this business of time. I do so because I feel that our mastery of this issue is a key to sensing what the secret Self is like. Our presence to the world is the crucial force here, and if we permit either past or future to cast their tyrannies over our project of self-discovery and -realization, we will not persist for long in the process of development.

The balance is crucial, and, for most of us, being in the present and being present to others is no easy accomplishment. But perhaps even more difficult is opening ourselves fully to experiences created out of the moment.

My own solution rests heavily on finding just the right relationship between waiting patiently and an act of will. In a specific way, this means relaxing and allowing myself to wait for inner direction, at the same time being ready to *be with* whatever image, idea, or memory comes into my present consciousness. Sometimes in the midst of relaxation, when my muscles are calm and the inner state slowed down, a single idea may drift into my awareness. Then I must hold it as best I can, letting it have its moment in the now. The result may be a discovery or a rediscovery of an inner truth which had stood clear of my straining consciousness.

Recently, while trying to pray, I found my mind clogged with past and future concerns. No matter how I tried, the tyrannies of past and future crowded my consciousness with guilt and anxiety, the two major emotions which come with being unavailable to the present. Then I let myself relax and waited. Soon my intellectual straining subsided and prayer became easy and simple and enlightening. Later, in reflecting on the happening, I wrote:

> Tonight
> I pray to Jesus
> as a child might do.
>
> Urgency
> gags sophistication;
> futility
> routs hard-won pride;
> desperation
> forces simple words
>
> Tonight
> I pray to Jesus
> as a child might do.[1]

[1]*United Methodists Today* (January, 1975), p. 37.

Soon afterward, I found myself reflecting on this experience of spontaneous prayer and many questions came tumbling into my consciousness: Why did I pray to Jesus? I never address my prayers to Jesus. Why such childlike words? Why not a curse instead of a prayer? And so it went—a long string of critical questions and comments having their roots in the past and the future.

During the moment of the experience, however, these critical tools were assigned to other time dimensions, and the *present* caught me in its creative matrix. True, the past was not eliminated, for the Jesus figure was selected to share in my immediate concerns, and images of the past helped me to create the present. But it was my openness to the present which brought discovery and release.

For those not comfortable with prayer or those who stand in another faith tradition, other images and thoughts may come into service, revealing pockets of the secret Self not previously known, or known differently.

In none of this, I hold, is it really necessary to go against reality—to "jump the track" of the world's time. In fact, the authenticity of being present in the creative now is often felt only in relation to reality.

5.
The Crucible of Reality

As I write these words, I am assuming that you have taken time out from your ordinary affairs to read this book. I am assuming that you have many responsibilities, that you probably need to work for a living, that at this very moment you could close the book and turn to a variety of activities that are part of your day-to-day life. You are not, my assumption runs, a professional mystic or a full-time adventurer of the spirit. I am inclined to think that you, like me, play many roles in life, are involved in earning a living, and spend considerable time working and playing in a world that is both exciting and mundane. Your interest in becoming more aware of the secret Self is in one sense avocational; the search may come to permeate all of life, but the process goes on alongside many other activities essential to your survival and well-being.

Before turning to my writing this morning, I had to drive my teen-age daughter to school. Then I took four cans of rubbish to the town dump, filled the car with gas, picked up my income tax forms, and made several telephone calls. I did these chores as part of my dealings with reality, for I, like you, am embedded in reality; and that reality does not always seem conducive to the psychospiritual project. Still, as I hope to show in this chapter, it is integral to the process of discovering the secret Self. It is, in fact, a desperately important part of the journey.

Facts and Metafacts

Most of us have no intention of living by facts alone. Indeed, the facts of reality are often colorless and dull. Important, yes; all-important, no.

One of the characteristics of the secret Self is its inclination to embrace metafacts, those meanings and extra perceptions which take you and me beyond the ordinary facts of reality. Indeed, one of the vocational hazards of the discovery of the secret Self is its magical feats, the way it can take an ordinary, dull fact and give it an extraordinary luster. But such magic does not just happen, nor is such a process without its dangers.

81

Before looking at a few specific illustrations of what this means in everyday life, we need to clarify the way in which we tend to view "reality." At one level, you may consider reality to be "what is *really* out there," what exists independently of your wishes and desires. As a friend of mine recently remarked, "Reality is *there,* man, no matter what you or I want to believe!" He was right, of course; but he oversimplified, as we are all inclined to do.

Alfred North Whitehead described the part of reality we call nature this way:

Nature gets credit which in truth should be reserved for ourselves, the rose for its scent, the nightingale for his song, the sun for its radiance. The poets are entirely mistaken. They should address their lyrics to themselves and should turn them into odes of self-congratulations on the excellence of the human mind. Nature is a dull affair, soundless, scentless, colorless, merely the hurrying of material, end-lessly, meaninglessly.

Yet in this morning's paper are many accounts of a reality which at least seems to exist beyond my perceptions and which is there despite my most intense longings to the contrary. I understand the philosopher's argument, but I feel deeply that it is inadequate. Facts and metafacts are related as fish are related to the waters in which they swim. But they are not the same, nor does one depend completely on the other for its identity.

At an experiential level, we are required to tell the

difference between facts and metafacts and to appreciate how making such differentiations can assist in discovering the secret Self.

Pause in your reading for a moment and ask yourself, "What facts am I aware of at this moment?" Can you not catalogue them, list them in some fashion, perhaps even write them down for another person to read?

Such descriptive facts, especially those close at hand, are not too difficult to identify. And despite their simplicity, they help to locate and control you. They have power. You had best treat such immediate and simple facts with respect.

The same is true, I claim, for the broad spectrum of facts which we call reality. Our task is to make continuous assessments of this complex web of factual data; and that is not nearly so easy as identifying simple facts close at hand.

Psychologists are fond of talking about "reality testing," by which they mean that the individual should try to determine how accurate his or her perceptions are. A young girl who considers herself unattractive is encouraged to check this out with others in a small group. A young man who considers himself bright enough to be a medical student is asked to take a series of intelligence tests. A middle-aged man who is depressed and says that he is worthless is asked to look critically at his past accomplishments. A great deal of counseling involves the checking and rechecking of personal perceptions against the claims of reality. Although such a process is at times painful, it is essential if we are to avoid false starts and wasted energy in the counseling process.

In the psychospiritual project a similar kind of assessment is needed. Where *in fact* are you right now?

I belabor this point because often I find people who are interested in the journey of self-discovery but do not have their feet firmly planted in reality. They do not seem to want to know where they are in terms of facts. For a variety of reasons—fear, shame, sense of inadequacy, for example—they do not wish to look clearly at the reality in which they are standing. Or, as some have discovered, they cannot do this fact-finding job alone. They need the help of a trusted guide— perhaps a counselor, a minister, a mental health professional, a teacher, a spiritual director.

Whatever the process—individual or social— coming to grips with reality is an important part of the psychospiritual project.

After all, reality—the complex web of facts— provides you with your resources for growth, just as it may limit you in that same growth process. Either way, reality is present and has power. To deny reality is to abort the project of discovering the secret Self.

Much of our resistance to facing facts can be overcome by thinking of them as givens without insisting that they be seen as "good" or "bad." The first task is to recognize them as present *with power*.

I know—it is a fact—that I am not handsome. It is a

fact that I am not rich. It is a fact that I am only moderately intelligent, neither brilliant nor stupid. It is a fact that I am middle-aged. It is a fact that I am white.

I might say, "I would be much further along in my understanding of the secret Self if I were a monk." Or I could argue, "I would be far more sensitive to the needs and limitations of others if I had not been an only child." Such observations are silly, although they may be true. The fact is that I am not a monk. The fact is that I am an only child. Both facts have power in them, and both can help me in my spiritual and psychological growth.

Indeed, the moment I realize this I have begun to move away from facts into metafacts. The realization, the full recognition of such descriptive facts is what is important. Acquiring the skills and sensitivities necessary to differentiate between facts and metafacts is an essential step in coming to the secret Self. Failure to make this elementary differentiation can discolor and distort the entire psychospiritual project.

How Should We View the Mundane?

Facts in themselves are often dull, descriptive, and lack movement. They bind us to earth, are ordinary, lack luster. They are, in a word, mundane. And yet it is the mundane that holds us in the world, keeps us "honest," prevents us from overeating the "pie in the sky," checks us when we run too fast or fly too high. In the psychospiritual project, it is the mundane which gives us the raw material from which to form creative syntheses of self-discovery.

How do you view the mundane? Balance here is vital, for the usual day-by-day realities with which we interact can deaden us to the realities of the secret Self. At the same time, these very factors can alert us to other dimensions of the secret Self. Deprivation, for instance, can be destructive and lead us away from the psychospiritual project. Yet it is quite possible that severe deprivation, including stark suffering, is capable of turning us inward in search of new and more profound meanings.

My own experience is that I move into the psychospiritual project more affirmatively when I give the mundane a chance to speak to me. Often the most common responsibility or chore takes on a glow when I really attend to it, let it speak fully to me, rather than resisting it or seeing it as a necessary evil.

Some years ago I came across a little book called *Kitchen Sonnets* in which the poet, a housewife, takes her everyday happenings and transforms them into exciting images and thoughts. She writes about doing dishes, marketing, hanging out the wash, canning vegetables, ironing, and dozens of other "mundane" events in her life. As an example, one of her poems reflects on what having children can mean:

He, who has children
Has other selves;
Tiny fragile selves
Built of his bones,
His flesh,
His pride,
His dreams;
Selves
Linking him to the beginning;
Fettering him to the silence
Beyond the end.[1]

Some may argue that this is flying in the face of reality, denying the hard, often painful and frustrating experiences of being a parent. Very well, if that is your choice in viewing the mundane. But I truly wonder whether the poet is not speaking more to my center in such thoughts than is the cynic or the so-called realist in reminding me only of the immediate and mundane aspects of child-rearing.

I wonder too whether investing myself in the mundane is not after all the best way of dealing with reality. By this I mean that when I stand out into reality I add part of myself to that reality, making it much more warm and meaningful. I am not simply an observer of the mundane then, but a real participant in it.

I come to see the mundane as part of me. I willingly take it in—fondle it, so to speak—and let it tell me

[1] Ethel Romig Fuller, *Kitchen Sonnets*, 3d ed. (Portland, Or.: Binfords & Mort, 1956).

something about the secret Self. In other words, I befriend it; and in that befriending a new kind of relationship comes into being.

The Art of Befriending

Befriending is a gentle art. Entered into clumsily, it can be little more than a superficial kind of "positive thinking," a mode doomed to an early abandonment. But practiced as a subtle and sensitive process, it can be the key to the psychospiritual project and to the discovery of the secret Self in all its intricate and amazing dimensions.

By befriending I mean that psychological process which allows me to own and even embrace many factors which at first may seem foreign to me and perhaps even negative in nature. It is a process which permits my center, the deepest and most central part of my self system, to affirm with integrity all that is truly a part of me. Such a principle allows me to recognize the basic goodness at the center of the Self.

The art of befriending starts with a quiet trust. You must come to believe that every characteristic which is authentically a part of you is *at center* good.

I know only too well the feelings and beliefs which are probably sweeping over you as you read these words. "How naïve!" "What foolishness!" "Wishful thinking!" "Uncritical romanticism!" "Unrealistic hogwash!"—these are the sorts of reactions which came to me again and again during the first months and years after I began the inner journey. They were the results of much living in a real world, and they had their roots in the judgments of many persons who had influenced me.

And I must admit that the full conviction that at its center the Self is essentially good did not get into my bones through my listening to sermons, reading books, or studying psychology—although such activities often presented me with the same teaching. I have no doubt that they helped me to understand this principle; but it was only through fair and at times troubled experiments that I came to own the reality of such a radical position.

At times the struggle to come to grips with the inner life is grim and dramatic, like Jacob's wrestling with the stranger. It can be an intense and powerful war, one which is capable of producing great inner turmoil. Who is this stranger with whom we must at times wrestle? What is this force that casts a dark shadow over the positive possibilities within? Humankind has speculated about such a battle since the beginning of consciousness.

Whether we see such a dynamic struggle in psychological or theological terms, the task for us as persons is to find the good that resides in the stranger, to become aware of the positive reality that moves through the darkest of our dreams and images. The most hideous of nightmares can carry a meaning for positive growth. The most negative of thoughts—real

89

dragons of destruction—can be domesticated and befriended.

Of course, the gentle art of befriending can be painful, and it can leave some real psychic scars. But experience after experience proves it to be an authentic project leading toward a true apprehension and appreciation of the secret Self.

How does one develop the art of befriending?

Here is where I find writing so inadequate. How much better it would be if I could be talking with you personally, could hear about your life, listen to the inflections in your voice, see the many stories in and around your eyes, sense the depth of your needs, get a hint of the power of your imagination. Then, perhaps, we could talk together about specific ways in which the befriending process could be developed.

I might suggest self-analysis as a start. Or I could talk about the need to keep a written journal of your psychospiritual moods, dreams, and ideas. Perhaps I would recommend counseling or psychotherapy. Or maybe I would encourage you to find a supportive group in which you would feel free to reveal some of the "dragons" kicking away in your unconscious. I might recommend some books that could get you started on the inner journey. Or I might suggest that you relate to a guide, someone in whom you could confide, who would help you hold up for gentle reflection those parts of yourself you are ready to examine trustfully.

One of these approaches, a combination of several,

or all of them together might be the right beginning for you. I do not know. My only certainty is that befriending can be learned and that it is an essential part of any psychospiritual project.

Perhaps a simple but true illustration will help you come to terms with the befriending principle.

This is the story of Gretchen, a twenty-eight-year-old woman who was just beginning to consider a life of prostitution and drugs. The only daughter of a somewhat stern midwestern family, Gretchen came east to the big city to earn a degree in journalism. As a teen-ager she had learned to win affection through sex. Since there was precious little acceptance or affection at home, Gretchen found it in the back seat of automobiles. In her hometown, she was seen as an easy mark sexually: once, while half-intoxicated, she "took on" more than half of the high school football team.

As a result of several circumstances, she decided to become a newspaperwoman. She saved enough money to get her through her first year of studies, won a small scholarship, and seemed to be making her way toward a career in journalism.

But Gretchen had developed a cynical set of beliefs about the world in general and men in particular, and she often found herself depressed and angry. She experimented with drugs, but she soon realized that they were essentially destructive and had only a passing influence on her moods. At the time that she was seriously considering turning to part-time prostitution "to cover academic expenses," she accidentally met another student who was in a charismatic group which met in a Roman Catholic church. Although she did not consider herself to be an especially religious person, she went with her friend one evening and was impressed with the sincerity and caring she found in the group. One of the members told her about counseling, suggesting that she might want to give it a try. Reluctantly, Gretchen went for an interview with a pastoral counselor who was also a psychologist.

At first she found little to talk about, but after a few weeks she began to tell the counselor about her sordid past, the sexual promiscuity, her deep hatred for men and for herself. It took several months for Gretchen to get the poison out. She painted a miserable self-portrait, claiming again and again that she was bad, rotten, horrible, dirty. Mostly the counselor just listened.

Then one day, nearly six months after she had started talking to the counselor, Gretchen paused in the midst of one of her self-criticisms and asked, "How do you manage to put up with me? Do you see something I don't?"

The counselor pointed a finger at Gretchen's midsection. "I see Gretchen who there in her center is good. I'm absolutely certain of that. From the first time we met, I felt your warmth. I was attracted to you. I liked you. The personal warmth that attracted me to you comes from the same source that makes sex so

92

easy for you to use and lets you know that you would have no trouble attracting customers. That warmth is what is deep within, a quality given to you. How will the center of Gretchen use that good—*that's* the issue."

This was a turning point in the relationship and in Gretchen's life. It took several more months, but finally she was able to feel and know—*really* feel and know—that at her center the quality that had led her to so many dark and negative beliefs about herself was in fact good and could be expressed in ways that were creative and growthful.

If Gretchen is reading this she will not need to be convinced that genuine befriending yields movement toward knowing the secret Self. I suspect, too, that she would agree that such a process is a subtle and artful one, which demands the maximum gentle care if it is to be genuine. And I am sure she would appreciate the fact that one's secret Self, especially at its center, can become so overlaid with false beliefs and cruel disillusionments that the bright vision is lost. It seems that only experience and experiment are capable of dissolving the negative crust built up by many years of saying *no* to the central region.

Owning the Reality You Are

Befriending implies embracement—owning all those aspects of the secret Self which we are able to allow into consciousness.

At the practical level, it means coming to the realization that I am able to own everything that helps to define me as a person—my body, my mind, my emotions. For Gretchen, it meant discovering a central region of goodness and recognizing that her feelings and behavior—good and bad—were hers, owned by the central region of the secret Self. These feelings and behavior no longer own her, as they did earlier in her life when she felt almost possessed. Of course, she still has feelings and temptations which could lead to trouble and dis-ease, but now she—her center—has come to own them in a peculiar and powerful way. They are hers to do with as she pleases.

I am personally convinced that one of the major factors preventing you and me from discovering the secret Self is that an encrustation of thoughts and beliefs, feelings and bodily needs, too often takes possession of the central region. Many of life's experiences, including much of society's expectations and demands, lay upon the secret Self layer after layer of false ideas, negative feelings, and views of the body and its needs.

Perhaps especially unfortunate is the fact that too often the first glimpses of this psychic and spiritual sabotage do not come until the second half of one's life. True, early childhood provides a kind of wise innocence which is very close to the sort of inner wisdom I am talking about, but it is soon dimmed under the onslaught of "reality" with its violent misperceptions and devious misleadings.

Still, I cannot help wondering and rejoicing at the resiliency of the human person. Our innate capacity to say *yes* to life long after the encrustation has seemingly calcified is quite amazing. Coming to own who you are in all your complexity and variety can take place even late in life and in the context of the most uncreative forces of reality. This seems to me something very close to a miracle.

6.
Centerpoint

Throughout this little manual I have talked about the central region of the person. I have written about the secret Self, and I have implied that there is in you and me a center, a quiet place that truly identifies you as you and me as me. I have tried to show that this center, once recognized and befriended, can be trusted. I hope I have said clearly and forcefully that choices and decisions made from this center will be growth-promoting and will contribute in a positive way to the psychospiritual project. I trust too that by such a claim I have suggested that motivations coming from "off-center"—especially those having their main roots in the opinions of others and in the conformity often inherent in much of reality—usually delay the expansion of consciousness and the owning of one's true identity.

In none of this, I realize, have I offered logically watertight arguments or philosophical proofs for anything. Although I know that each sentence in the above paragraph could be challenged with extensive intellectual arguments, I am asking you to *experience* these suggestions rather than to argue about them.

I am not trying to be anti-intellectual in suggesting that you discover your center through experience. I am merely trying to hold to my original intention of sharing with you informally what I sense about the nature of the secret Self and about the ways leading to its center. The fact is that in my own life I have found that my technical studies in psychology, philosophy, and theology have often prevented me from coming to a genuine awareness of my center rather than guiding me to it. I love to read and to study, and I find the intellectual mode to be a stimulating and exciting part of my life. But I have learned, especially in recent years, that when it comes to the psychospiritual project, such an intellectual approach can be distracting and even abortive. The intellectual format, including the great reliance on reason and logic, often represents just another layer of encrustation piled atop the secret Self.

Centerpoint, I am suggesting, is greater and deeper than your critical faculties. You may come to own your intellectual tendencies and abilities, even to value them highly, but they are not you—they are not the central point of your secret Self.

Of course, I realize that even in the process of becoming aware of the secret Self, you, like me, may want to reflect on and to understand what is happening and why. My plea is that you let the experiencing of discovery have first priority, at least while you are on this particular journey where the secret Self is allowed to become the dominant and most precious objective.

Centerpoint Without Idolatry

Does the suggestion that one should experience without understanding seem extreme? Does it in fact sound as if I am making the secret Self into a god? Is this not a form of idolatry?

Idolatry is often thought of when one elevates a preliminary concern to ultimacy. I suppose it would indeed be possible to believe that the secret Self is of ultimate concern, and if I believed this, and at the same time were committed to some meaning system which claimed some other object as being of ultimate concern, I would be practicing idolatry. But, of course, I do not make any such claim about the secret Self, nor, I suspect, do you.

Without even raising the issue of the existence or reality of a deity, I am aware that there is much in my life which I value above the secret Self. As I write these words this morning I can see my thirteen-year-old son playing with his painted turtles on the sundeck. His blond hair, his body, his voice all tell me that I value him above my center. I really do. And I am sure that you can say the same, even if you are committed to the psychospiritual project with deep vigor.

No, the project of discovering the secret Self is not in itself idolatrous. I do believe it to be a preliminary concern—but by this I mean that it may well be a necessary prerequisite for making valuations of what indeed is ultimate. Put bluntly, the centerpoint process may precede any genuine attempt to come to terms with some ultimate meaning or some final object of devotion. To bypass the central region of the secret Self and claim authentic understanding of a larger reality is, I believe, quite difficult, perhaps impossible.

So do not let the accusation that the psychospiritual project is idolatrous keep you from beginning the journey. And do not let the claim that such a concern is "egocentric" dampen your motivation. I think there is much evidence to suggest otherwise, and that such criticisms often arise out of misunderstandings and fear—part of the encrustation forming around the secret Self.

Sensing the Unmanifest

Although I believe that the project of discovering the secret Self is a preliminary to discovering wider realities, I have found that sensing that there is a great deal more unknown than known can nurture the development of the psychospiritual project.

My suggestion is that the conviction that reality is far more unmanifest than manifest carries with it some very important consequences, and that these consequences have far-reaching implications for you and me in our journey inward. The two most important consequences have to do with the process of humility and the dynamics of search.

I have observed that those persons who believe that the world of the unmanifest is considerably greater than the world of the manifest are apt to walk more gently and to relate to others more profoundly than those persons preoccupied primarily with the manifest. This sort of mind-set might be called humility, in the sense that it promotes a spirit of expectation before that which gives itself to us. Although we come to know more and more of the unmanifest, we are not the creators of this unknown and mysterious continent. The unmanifest has given itself to us before, and to others in the past, and therefore we intuitively know that it will do so again and again. An active kind of waiting becomes part of the life-style of those who sense the unmanifest.

Equally important, it seems to me, is the psycholog-

100

ical principle that such a recognition of the magnitude and power of the unmanifest leads us to a stance of searching. As long as you believe that there is more to come than has yet come, you will involve yourself in the searching process. I believe, in fact, that this dynamic is at the heart of all true religion and science and that it is a crucial motivational principle in the psychospiritual project.

The opposite of this sense of the unmanifest is often a form of arrogance. And certainly, arrogance, when present, can disrupt and short-circuit any genuine movement toward the secret Self.

Perhaps this is why so many of the great mystics and spiritual leaders of the past considered spiritual pride the most vicious enemy to the development of the spiritual life. As St. John of the Cross once wrote, "When beginners become aware of their own fervour and diligence in their spiritual works and exercises, this propensity of theirs gives rise to secret pride . . . they conceive a certain satisfaction in the contemplation of their works and of themselves."

My impression is that this same dynamic—whether we call it spiritual pride or not—is at work whenever we allow ourselves to believe that we know more than there is to know. This is an especially dangerous temptation very soon after we have said *yes* to the invitation to begin the inner journey. I have found in myself a tendency toward great enthusiasm whenever I sense that I have tasted a bit of the secret Self. At times this enthusiasm wants to say, "Look, those of

101

you who have not said *yes,* don't you see how foolish you are in living off-center? You poor, deluded cripples, can't you see how sublime and whole the secret Self is?" Fortunately, such thoughts are rarely expressed; and, just as fortunately, they come less and less frequently with each realization that the more I come to know the secret Self the more I see how much is still left to befriend.

Have you ever read a letter you wrote twenty years ago? Have you ever reflected seriously on some belief you held with arrogant vigor when you were much younger? I sometimes go back and reread a book or an article I wrote two decades ago, and often I cannot help asking, "Did I really write *that*?"

Life is full of examples which should help us to view our present situation with gentle humor. I am sure that some of you reading this simple observation about how we change may be thinking, "How naïve this man is! Why, I knew that a lifetime ago!" But we do tend to forget the subtle ripples of change. Our organism has a way of making us think that we have always felt and thought as we do right now. As I see my hand holding the pen, I cannot recall what that same hand looked like when it held a pen in grade school back in eastern Pennsylvania. Even my handwriting, I tend to believe, has not changed—until I pull some of my early compositions from an attic trunk!

When we are truthful with ourselves, we get a glimpse of the fact that life can be an unending movement toward maturity and even wisdom. If that principle can be held firmly in mind, it is really difficult to be arrogant or foolish in our claims. The center of the secret Self comprehends this fully; it is a trusted piece of knowledge.

Perhaps what I have been saying in this section is what I said in the second chapter: life is a mystery to be lived. It is this authentic appreciation of mystery—both within me and beyond me—which tends to dissolve spiritual pride and which motivates me for additional search. A sense of the unmanifest not only makes my psychospiritual project important but it makes it necessary—a call I can hardly refuse to hear or to answer.

This search, of course, can take many forms, and we come to it from a variety of perspectives. At times it comes upon us as a surprise, at other times as a necessity. Perhaps the search takes on a rather formal, intellectual mode, leading us to the study of wisdom literature, to the examination of philosophical or theological books and arguments, to the critical assessment or reassessment of religious dogma and convictions. At other times it comes upon us in a much more personal mode, leading us to self-analysis, to psychological befriending, to a new style of openness to the inner world.

In this book, I have placed considerable emphasis on the personal mode—not in any way to minimize the formal and intellectual mode of search. There is need for a vital rhythm here, a kind of art in moving back and forth between formal and personal search, keeping both in balance in accordance with the state of the secret Self at the time.

In my own case, I believe the formal-intellectual mode has tended to be intrusive and at times dominating. Such a mode can be an easy defense against the search which stresses the personal and which finds its main focus for meanings within the person, at the very center of the secret Self.

Nurturing the Centerpoint Process

Living from the center is a subtle and challenging art form, one which requires us to engage in a never-ending way of life that is a combination of gentle waiting and persistent search. Like so many other important projects, the psychospiritual one requires your attention just as surely as does a project of physical conditioning or weight control or learning a foreign language.

Nurturing the centerpoint process is a lot like tending a garden. In essence the growth of plants is a natural process determined by a variety of forces that are beyond the gardener's control. Nevertheless, there are some activities on the part of the gardener which are crucial to growth.

Again, I must in all honesty say—although by now I

am sure that my warning will be irritating to you—that nurturing is a highly individual affair. The specifics must be developed in creative relation to those genotypic and phenotypic characteristics which are peculiarly yours and in terms of where you are in your own development.

About all I can do in this final section is to share with you some of the major nurturing activities which I have found especially necessary in my own movement toward center and in my own assessment of the centering process.

The first activity which I have found helpful is reading. I have been an avid reader for most of my life. Although much of my reading time is vocational in the sense that books are as much tools for the professor as wrenches are for the mechanic, reading in relation to the psychospiritual project extends beyond this somewhat formal activity. In this regard, I find the reading of poetry especially relevant in that certain kinds of poetry frequently center on the reality which rests below the surface. In poetry's hints and its attempts to make man plain I often find a kind of honesty quite removed from the sham present in much ordinary encounter. Poetry, especially confessional poetry, relates me to kindred spirits and helps me to realize that there is a community of searchers "out there" who sense and try to share an inner world somewhat akin to mine.

Another kind of reading I have found helpful, even necessary, is what might be called devotional or spiritual literature. I am referring to books and articles which are specifically directed at the development of psychological and spiritual qualities. This sort of reading provides me with inspiration and guidance, especially during those inevitable periods when the movement toward the secret Self seems to come to a near standstill. For me such reading is essential to carry me through these dry spells.

A second activity which I find to be nurturing to the inner project is writing. I am especially aware of the importance of keeping some sort of journal, a running account of my inner life, my dreams, and my fantasies. Although I do not tie myself to my psychospiritual journal and do not whip myself into making entries on any kind of rigid schedule, I do treat the journal as a friend to whom I go whenever I feel there is something important to say. I find it helpful to put into writing those thoughts and feelings which have come to me during my waking and sleeping hours. When I am deeply troubled or angered by outward circumstances, for example, I find that writing down the events helps me to stand back from them and to sense more clearly whether my attitudes and behavior are rooted in my center or are coming from off-center. There is something about the writing process itself which guides me in this sort of evaluation, especially when I allow myself to write freely and openly.

Because I have been writing since my teen-age days, I find other kinds of writing—poems, stories, articles—equally helpful in clarifying my inner dynamics. For many years I did not fully appreciate this rich form of self-expression, because I let it be overly influenced by a need to be published. I found that I was writing a poem or a story *for publication,* and this fact alone seemed to drain out the juices that gave real growth to the inner project. I do not mean by this that writing for publication automatically runs counter to the use of writing as part of the psychospiritual project. But my observation is that the kind of writing which nurtures my centering process is not always the kind of writing which is publishable. For me, writing in itself is growth-producing. If such writing finds its way into print and can be shared with others, I am delighted. If not, I am no longer crushed—for the activity itself has already yielded considerable insight and guidance.

A third nurturing activity is physical work and recreation. I realize that placing these together may seem strange, especially to those of you who earn your living by physical labor. Probably you would be inclined to place physical work and recreation in quite different camps.

This morning, before starting my writing stint, I had a cup of coffee and a doughnut in a local cafe where the town's firemen, custodians, and mechanics tend to gather. Just looking at the hands on the counter revealed the difference between those who do physical labor continuously and the "professor" who works mostly with mind and book. The hands of the laborers were generally larger and stronger, pocked by the knocks of hammers and wrenches, even darkly engrained with the stubborn grime of machines. For most of them, I'm sure, recreation would be seen as a release from physical toil.

For me, however, the distinction fades. Physical labor in mid-morning after two hours of writing may come as a form of recreation. Perhaps the important point is that physical activity, whether "work" or "fun," is, within my particular life-style, a nurturing process itself. To exert myself physically does more than remind me that I have a body; it offers me a chance to feel that body in a peculiar or different way. Put simply, when I am "out of shape" physically, my psychospiritual project tends to reflect that fact.

Now, I am not in any sense a nut on physical fitness, but I have learned that part of the secret Self is intimately related to my body and its processes. Indeed, I have discovered again and again that when I neglect my body and permit it to become overly flabby, I tend to act and feel off-center. Although I have not as yet identified any specific formula or even determined "which comes first," I am certain that when the psychospiritual project is faltering I am usually in need of some sort of physical activity.

Finally, I have found that nurturing the centering process can be greatly facilitated with the help of a guide. Although my own genotypic and phenotypic forces tend to make me an individualist and even a loner, I am conscious that relating to at least one other

108

person as part of the inner journey is a desirable form of nurturing. Again, I realize the personal nature of this preference, recognizing that you may not find this as essential as I do. It may be that you, like many persons I know, will find it more helpful to be in some sort of group setting or to belong to a fellowship of some kind. In my own case, however, and at this point in my own psychospiritual project, I find a guide—a person more advanced in the process of actualizing the secret Self than I—of great value.

I see this guide infrequently—perhaps monthly or every other month, depending on a variety of circumstances. Right now my thought is that my guide gives me something like a "five-thousand-mile check," and offers me a safe and trusting relationship in which I can move a bit closer to my center and have such movement evaluated by a person who is both more objective and at the same time more accomplished than I.

Needless to say, the selection of a guide is exceedingly important.

These four activities—reading, writing, physical labor-recreation, and the guidance of another person—I find to be especially helpful in nurturing the centering process. But these are only my findings. In your own psychospiritual project you will surely discover others of equal or greater help to you; and you will probably find that some of mine are not worth very much.

Traveling to the secret Self is a truly *unique* adventure, perhaps the only one left in our modern world of conformity with its demand for public expression. And it is yours to develop in ways that are truly yours and yours alone.